ESSENTIAL KEYBOARD REPERTOIRE

100 EARLY INTERMEDIATE SELECTIONS
IN THEIR ORIGINAL FORM
Baroque to Modern

SELECTED AND EDITED BY
LYNN FREEMAN OLSON

A cassette (#4057) or CD (#4059)
recording of the selections contained in
Essential Keyboard Repertoire, Volume 1,
beautifully played by Kim O'Reilly,
is available separately.

Second Edition
Copyright © MCMXCV by Alfred Publishing Co., Inc.
All rights reserved. Printed in USA.

Cover design: Martha Widmann   Art direction: Ted Engelbart

FOREWORD

Ever since the time when keyboard instruments first appeared, there has been a natural tendency to provide materials specifically for pupils who are beginning to explore a musical path on those instruments and for the teachers who become their important guides. In every period teachers have arisen to help continue the culture by demonstrating a way to acquire musical skills and express them at the keyboard. These same teachers have required (and often created) materials that could make such basic instruction possible, meaningful, and pleasurable.

We are the fortunate recipients of this historical stream, one that flows on today. The storehouse of keyboard repertoire for learning purposes has become so vast that were each teacher today forced to sift through all the available materials, and then authenticate their editions, the lessons themselves might never begin! Thus evolve albums such as the one you hold now. The essentials are here—those basic materials proven effective over years of teaching experience. You will recognize some of the bread-and-butter pieces at once; but now they appear in the clearest printing and layout possible and with contents and an index to locate works by title as well as by composer. The format avoids page turns almost entirely.

You see before you a traditional musical garden. It is planted here and there with some welcome surprises, and these, together with our choice of the perennials, make this landscape our very own, designed with both beauty and usefulness in mind.

EDITING

All pieces occur in their original forms—no notes added or removed. Where articulations have been added, you are always informed. In much of the music through the eighteenth century, dynamics and musical directions have been selected editorially, and these always appear in brackets. The fingering throughout is based on modern teaching principles and is that of the editor.

SEQUENCE

With few exceptions (because of page-turn considerations), the book is organized historically by composer birth date. Within each composer grouping the works are presented, as much as possible, in order of difficulty.

One major exception to this plan is the appearance of pieces from the *Notebook for Anna Magdalena Bach*. We have chosen the date on the book's original cover (1725) to decide the position of all selections from it. Research reveals that the authorship of many of these pieces cannot be determined; on the other hand, we now know the composer identity for certain selections, many of which have appeared on programs for years as being composed by J. S. Bach. Sebastian himself most certainly did not compose these familiar short dances which are of a later style than his own works. He inaugurated the gift booklet for his wife by copying into it some of his own compositions, but from there on the contents were largely the province of Anna Magdalena, her family, and their friends.

LEVEL

A few of the very easiest pieces of repertoire commonly taught were found to be too simple for this book, but, in general, you will discover that the collection carries the student through the first stages of acquaintance with authentic repertoire.

As a studio aid here is a selection of perhaps the dozen easiest pieces from which one might choose to begin:

Telemann	*Fantasia*	10
Rameau	*Menuet en Rondeau*	14
Wagenseil	*Menuet*	22
L. Mozart	*Minuet*	23
Duncombe	*Sonatina*	39
Türk	*Arioso*	56
Beethoven	*Russian Folksong*	70
Le Couppey	*Musette*	94
Köhler	*Soldier's Song*	95
Gurlitt	*Badinage*	96
Kabalevsky	*Scherzo*	125
Shostakovich	*March*	140

Now please enjoy these most beautiful pages of essential beginning musical expressions from our keyboard heritage.

Lynn Freeman Olson

4

CONTENTS

Menuet

JEAN-BAPTISTE LULLY
(1632–1687)

Minuet

JOHANN KRIEGER
(1651–1735)

The slur indications are editorial.

The Little Trifle

(LE PETIT RIEN)

FRANÇOIS COUPERIN
(1668–1733)

The slur groupings are editorial.

Fantasia

GEORG PHILIPP TELEMANN
(1681–1767)

Minuet

GEORG PHILIPP TELEMANN

Fantasia

GEORG PHILIPP TELEMANN

Slur groupings are editorial.

Menuet en Rondeau

JEAN PHILIPPE RAMEAU
(1683–1764)

The Fifers

JEAN-FRANÇOIS DANDRIEU
(1682–1738)

* All eighth notes may be played semi-detached.

Minuet

JOHANN SEBASTIAN BACH
(1685–1750)

Passepied

GEORGE FRIDERIC HANDEL
(1685–1759)

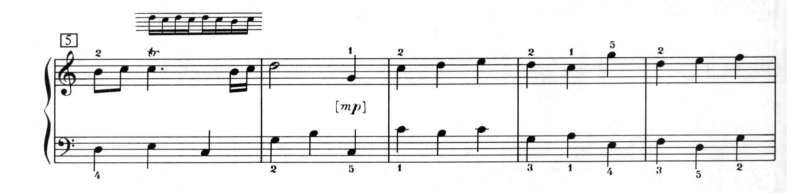

Bourrée

GEORGE FRIDERIC HANDEL

Minuet

CARLOS SEIXAS *
(1704–1742)

* Pronounced "say-shus".
The articulation is editorial.

Minuet

WILHELM FRIEDEMANN BACH
(1710–1784)

Menuet

GEORG CHRISTOPH WAGENSEIL
(1715–1777)

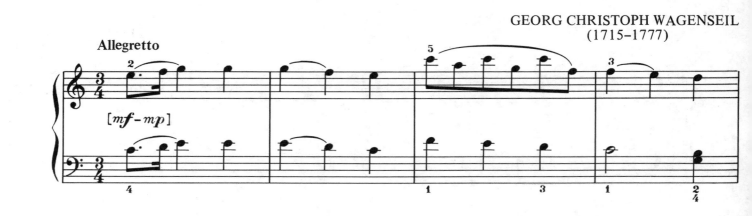

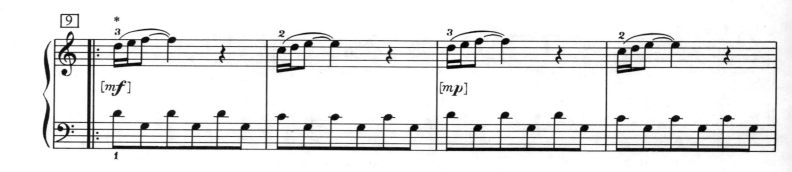

* These figures represent a written out ornamentation.

Minuet

from *Notebook for Wolfgang*

LEOPOLD MOZART
(1719–1787)

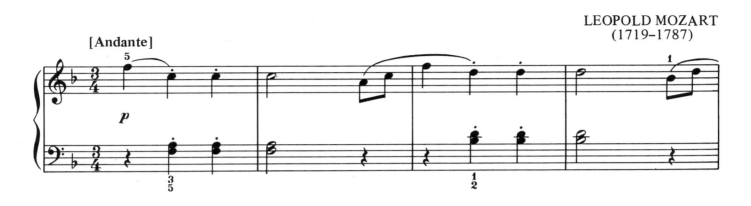

Minuet

from *Notebook for Wolfgang*

LEOPOLD MOZART

Minuet

from *Notebook for Nannerl*

LEOPOLD MOZART

[Moderato]

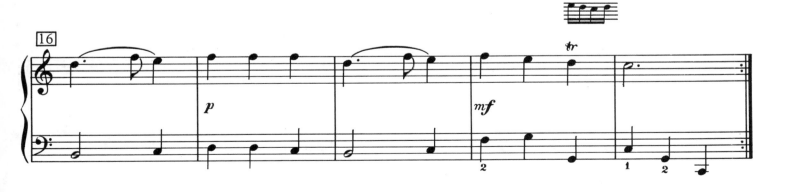

Bourlesq

from *Notebook for Wolfgang*

LEOPOLD MOZART

Polonaise

from the *Notebook for Anna Magdalena Bach*
(1725)

ANONYMOUS

Menuet

from the *Notebook for Anna Magdalena Bach*
(1725)

ANONYMOUS

Menuet

from the *Notebook for Anna Magdalena Bach*
(1725)

CHRISTIAN PETZOLD**

[Moderato]

* For ease, rapid ornaments may be omitted.
** Now known as the composer; formerly anonymous.

Musette

from the *Notebook for Anna Magdalena Bach*
(1725)

ANONYMOUS

The eighth notes throughout may be played slightly detached.

34

Marche

from the *Notebook for Anna Magdalena Bach*
(1725)

CARL PHILIPP EMANUEL BACH

Menuet

from the *Notebook for Anna Magdalena Bach*
(1725)

CHRISTIAN PETZOLD

Menuet

from the *Notebook for Anna Magdalena Bach*
(1725)

ANONYMOUS

Sonatina

WILLIAM DUNCOMBE
(1690–1769)

Fanfare Minuet

WILLIAM DUNCOMBE

German Dance

FRANZ JOSEPH HAYDN
(1732–1809)

German Dance

FRANZ JOSEPH HAYDN

German Dance

FRANZ JOSEPH HAYDN

Gypsy Dance

FRANZ JOSEPH HAYDN

Some articulation has been chosen to be consistent with Haydn's style.

German Dance

FRANZ JOSEPH HAYDN

* L.H. detached throughout.

Minuetto

JOHANN CHRISTIAN BACH/
FRANCO PASQUALE RICCI "METHOD"

The slurs are editorial aids.

Minuet

from *Guida di Musica*

JAMES HOOK
(1746–1827)

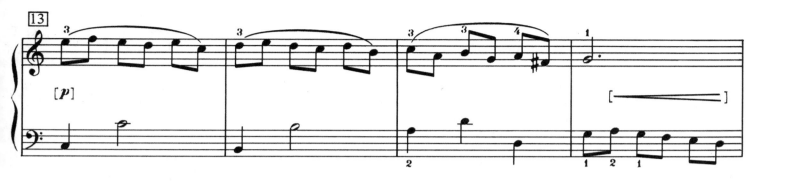

Scherzando

JOHANN FRIEDRICH REICHARDT
(1752–1814)

52

Valse

MUZIO CLEMENTI
(1752–1832)

Risoluto

JOHANN CHRISTIAN BACH/
FRANCESCO PASQUALE RICCI "METHOD"

Risoluto [Allegro moderato]

Arioso

DANIEL GOTTLOB TÜRK
(1756–1813)

Rondino

DANIEL GOTTLOB TÜRK

The Hunting Horns and the Echo

DANIEL GOTTLOB TÜRK

Never a Dull Moment

DANIEL GOTTLOB TÜRK

Minuet

WOLFGANG AMADEUS MOZART, K. 6
(1756–1791)

Minuet

WOLFGANG AMADEUS MOZART, K. 2

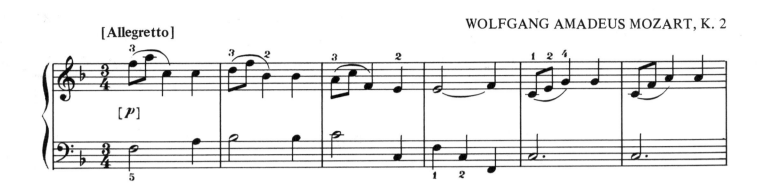

Allegro

WOLFGANG AMADEUS MOZART, K. 3

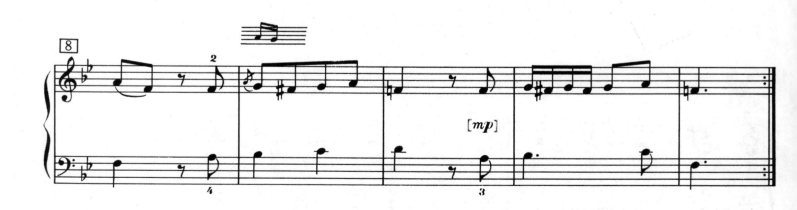

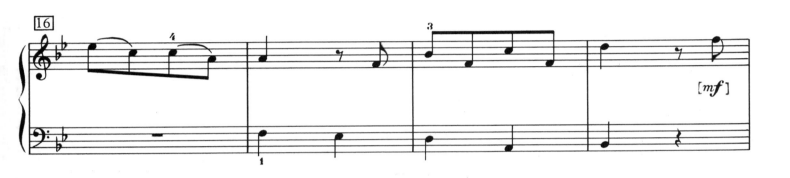

Minuet and Trio

WOLFGANG AMADEUS MOZART, K. 1

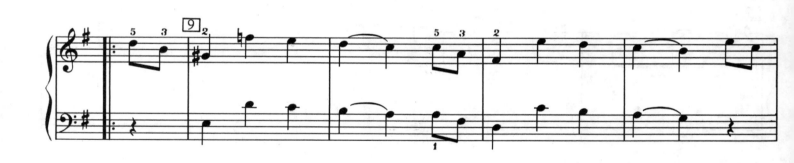

Trio

Dance

CHRISTIAN GOTTLOB NEEFE
(1748–1798)

Allegretto scherzando

[*detached*]

The title has been added, and articulation and dynamics made consistent to style.

Entrée

IGNAZ JOSEPH PLEYEL
(1757–1831)

Adagio

DANIEL STEIBELT
(1765–1823)

Russian Folk Song

(Theme from Variations for Violin and Piano)

LUDWIG van BEETHOVEN, Op. 107, No. 7
(1770–1827)

Russian Folk Song

("Little Minka")

LUDWIG van BEETHOVEN

Écossaise

LUDWIG van BEETHOVEN

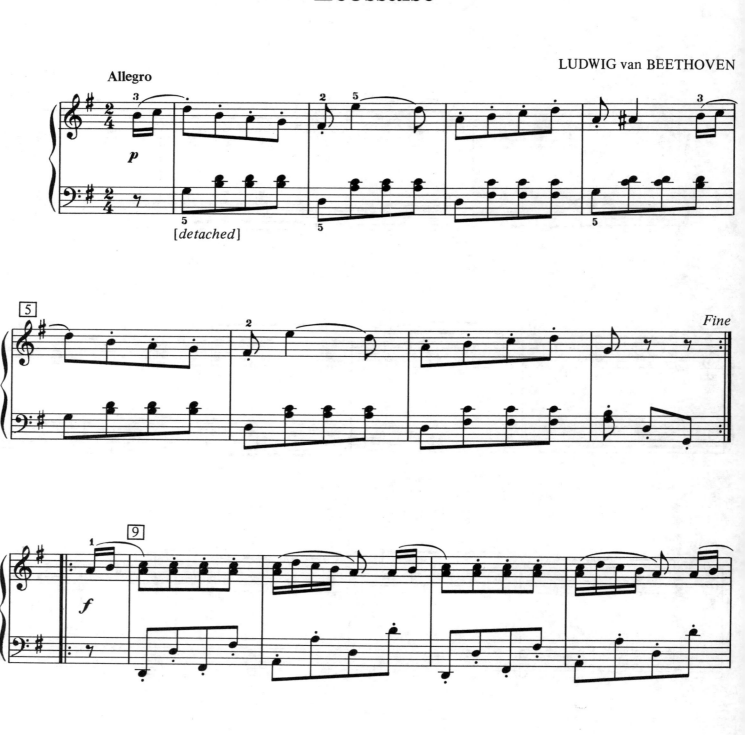

German Dance

LUDWIG van BEETHOVEN

German Dance

LUDWIG van BEETHOVEN

German Dance

LUDWIG van BEETHOVEN

German Dance

LUDWIG van BEETHOVEN

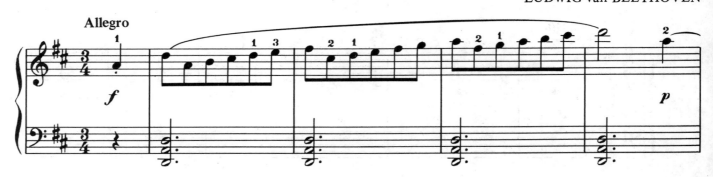

Allemande

CARL CZERNY
(1791–1857)

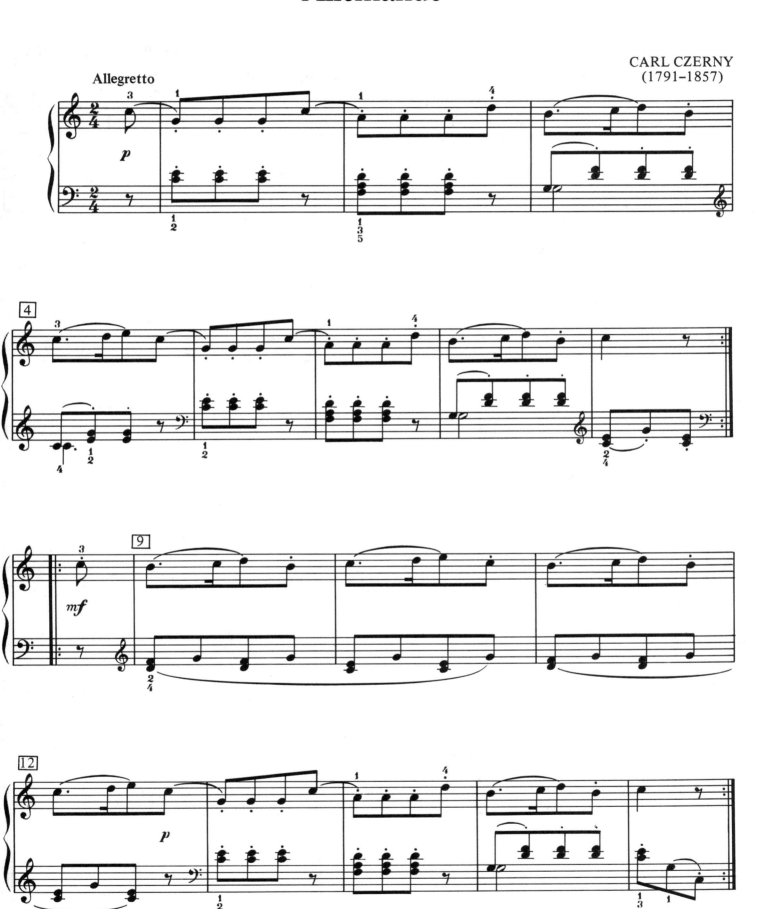

Écossaise

FRANZ SCHUBERT
(1797–1828)

Écossaise

FRANZ SCHUBERT

Etude

JEAN-BAPTISTE DUVERNOY, Op. 176, No. 24
(1800–1880)

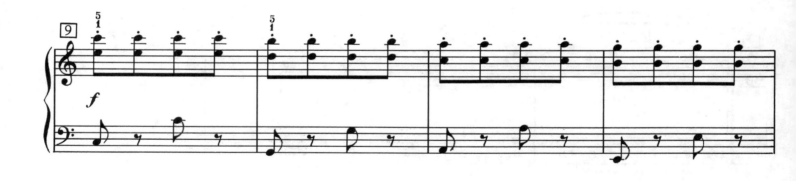

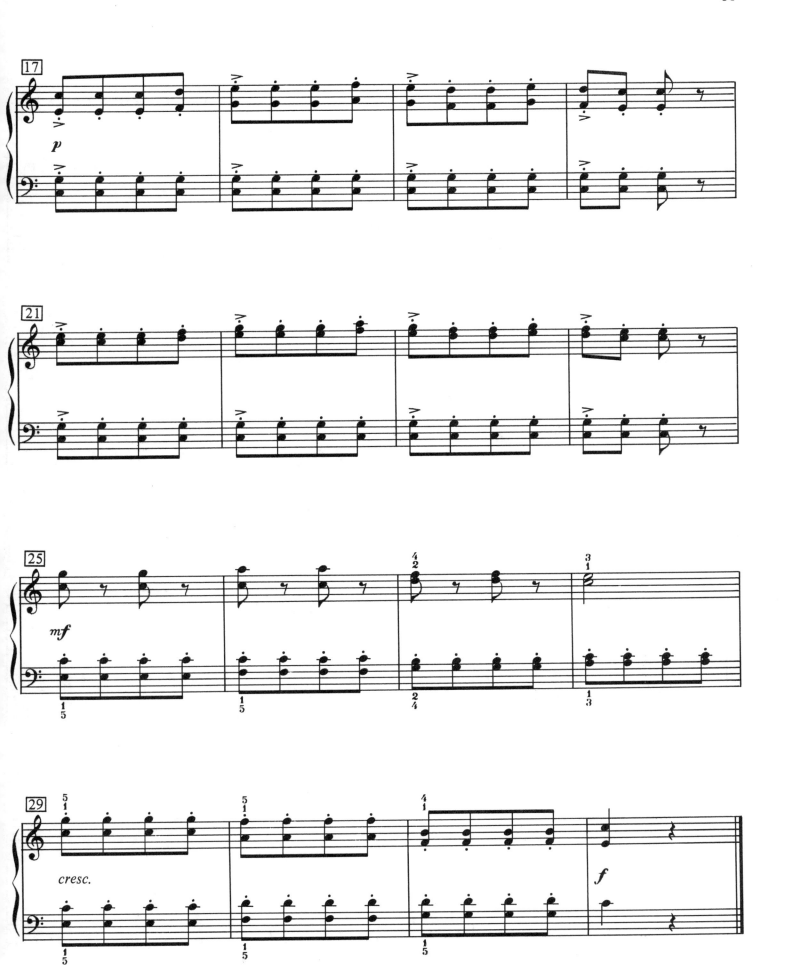

Etude

GIUSEPPE CONCONE, Op. 24, No. 8
(1801–1861)

Andantino un poco mosso

staccato sempre

Arabesque

JOHANN FRIEDRICH BURGMÜLLER, Op. 100, No. 2
(1806–1874)

Allegro scherzando

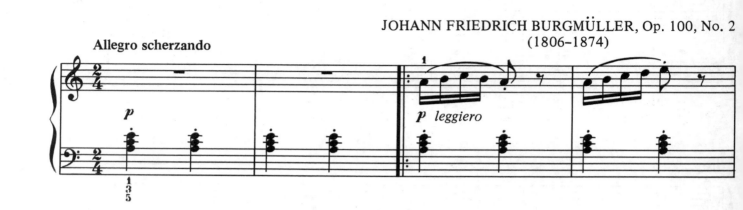

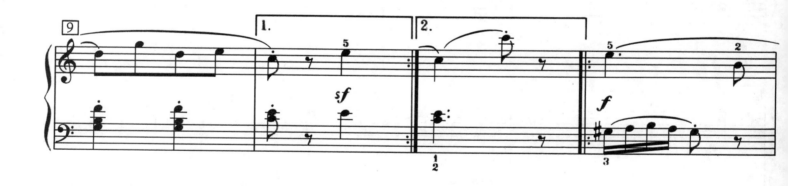

Soldiers' March

from *Album for the Young*

ROBERT SCHUMANN, Opus 68, No. 2
(1810–1856)

* Schumann used *f* to indicate an accent in this piece.

Wild Rider

from *Album for the Young*

ROBERT SCHUMANN, Opus 68, No. 8

* Contrast added to the return in measure 17.

89

Melody

from *Album for the Young*

ROBERT SCHUMANN, Op. 68, No. 1

Etude

FELIX LE COUPPEY, Op. 17, No. 6
(1811–1887)

Musette

FELIX LE COUPPEY

Soldier's Song

LOUIS KÖHLER
(1820–1886)

Badinage

CORNELIUS GURLITT, Op. 197
(1820–1901)

Morning Greeting

CORNELIUS GURLITT, Op. 130, No. 1

Some slurs added for style consistency.

Etude

CORNELIUS GURLITT

Allegro non troppo

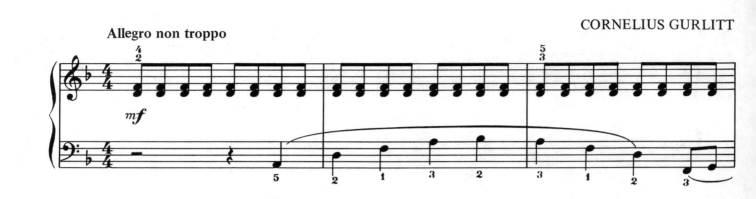

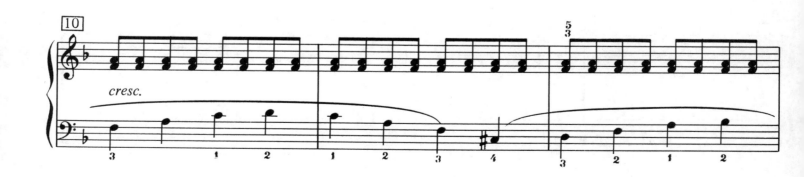

Scherzo

CORNELIUS GURLITT

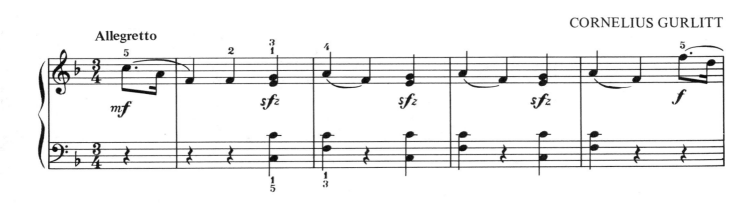

The Little Prankster

CORNELIUS GURLITT, Op. 117, No. 18

Prayer

CORNELIUS GURLITT

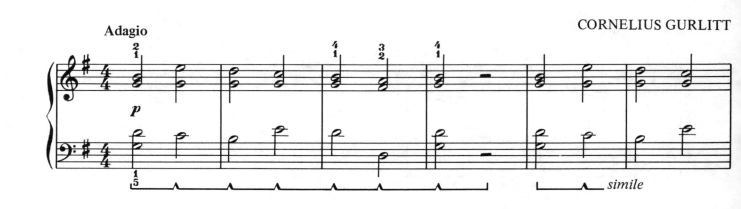

The pedaling is editorial.

Hunting Music

CORNELIUS GURLITT, Op. 210, No. 5

A Little Flower

Allegretto grazioso

CORNELIUS GURLITT, Op. 205, No. 11

The pedaling is editorial.

In Church

PETER ILYICH TCHAIKOVSKY
(1840–1893)

Nostalgic Song

ALEXANDER GRETCHANINOV, Op. 98
(1864–1956)

The Bear

VLADIMIR REBIKOV
(1866–1920)

The Clown

VLADIMIR REBIKOV

Playing Soldiers

VLADIMIR REBIKOV, Op. 31, No. 4

Tale

SAMUIL MAYKAPAR
(1867–1938)

Autumn

Andantino

SAMUIL MAYKAPAR

Ped. simile

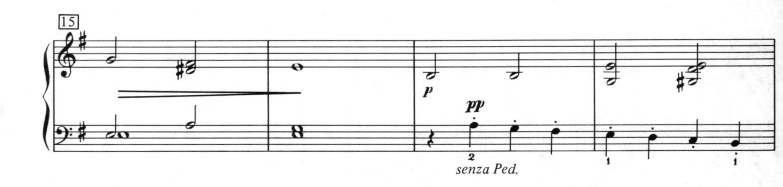

senza Ped.

Scherzino

SAMUIL MAYKAPAR

Hungarian Folk Song

from *The First Term at the Piano*

BÉLA BARTÓK
(1881–1945)

Minuet

from *The First Term at the Piano*

BÉLA BARTÓK

Song

("Come home, Lidi")

from *For Children*

BÉLA BARTÓK

Play Song

from *For Children*

BÉLA BARTÓK

Poco allegretto

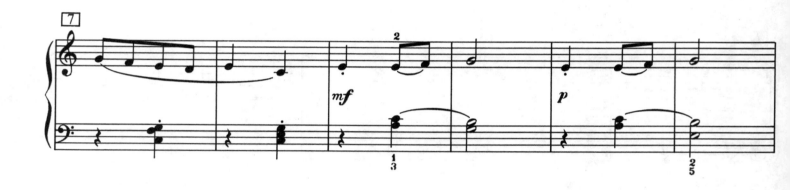

Più mosso

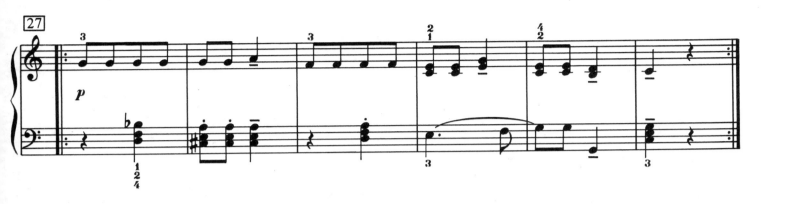

Folk Dance
("Hey there, tulip!")
from *For Children*

BÉLA BARTÓK

Song

("So small is the street of Istvánd")

from *For Children*

BÉLA BARTÓK

Scherzo

from *24 Pieces for Children*

DMITRI KABALEVSKY, Op. 39, No. 12
(1904–1987)

Jumping

from *24 Pieces for Children*

DMITRI KABALEVSKY, Op. 39, No. 15

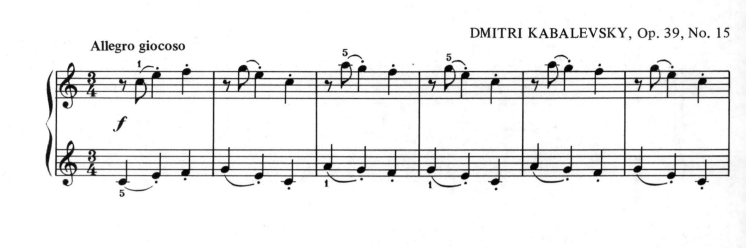

Folk Dance

from *24 Pieces for Children*

DMITRI KABALEVSKY, Op. 39, No. 17

Little Song

from *30 Pieces for Children*

DMITRI KABALEVSKY, Op. 27, No. 2

Waltz

from *24 Pieces for Children*

DMITRI KABALEVSKY, Op. 39, No. 13

Toccatina

from *30 Pieces for Children*

DMITRI KABALEVSKY, Op. 27, No. 12

Clowns

from *24 Pieces for Children*

DMITRI KABALEVSKY, Op. 39, No. 20

Brief Story

from *24 Pieces for Children*

DMITRI KABALEVSKY, Op. 39, No. 22

Little Fable

from *30 Pieces for Children*

DMITRI KABALEVSKY, Op. 27, No. 9

Allegro moderato

Variations on a Russian Folk Song

DMITRI KABALEVSKY, Op. 51, No. 1

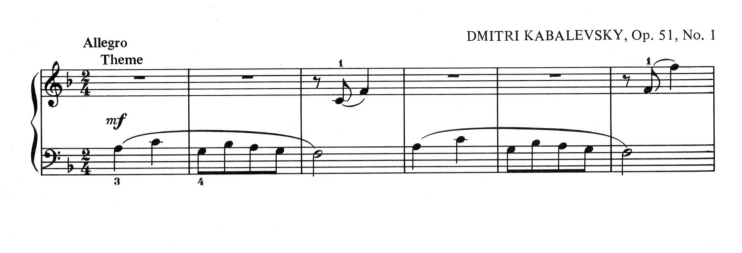

138

March

DMITRI SHOSTAKOVICH
(1906–1975)

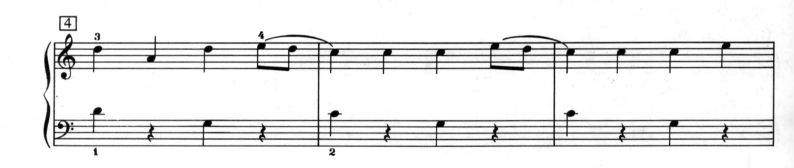

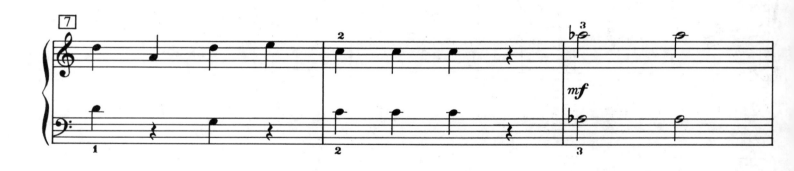

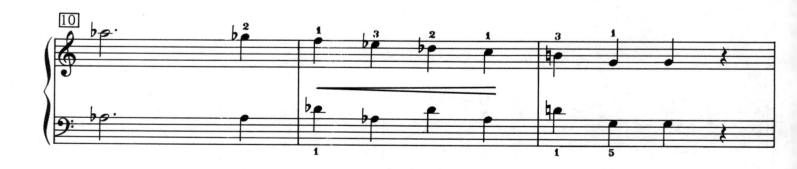

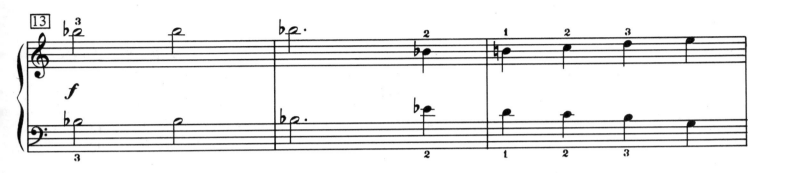

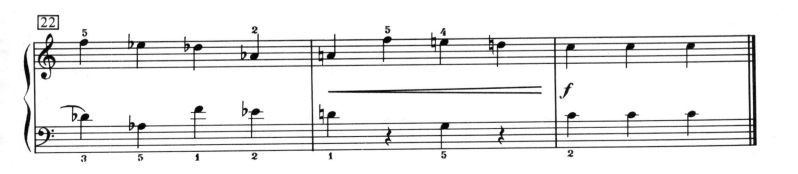

INDEX

ABOUT THIS EDITION

Alfred has made every effort to make this book not only attractive, but more convenient and long-lasting as well. Most books larger than 96 pages do not lie flat or stay open easily. In addition, the pages in these books (which are usually glued together) tend to break away from the spine after repeated use.

In Alfred's special **lay-flat binding** editions for large books, pages are sewn together in multiples of 16, preventing pages from falling out of the book while still allowing it to stay open easily. Alfred also offers another type of special binding for large books called **plastic comb binding**. This format allows the book to lie open even flatter than the lay-flat binding.

We hope that these long-lasting, convenient bindings will encourage additional use of our publications and will continue to bring added pleasure to you for years to come.